Rambles

Also by Beatriz Copello and published by Ginninderra Press

Witches, Women & Words

No Salami Fairy Bread

Beatriz Copello

Rambles

GP

Rambles
ISBN 978 1 76109 599 3

Cover image: Beatriz Copello

First published 2023 by
GINNINDERRA PRESS
PO Box 3461 Port Adelaide 5015
www.ginninderrapress.com.au

Contents

Animalia Decimati

flank of dog in kimchi sauce
dolphins wrapped in plastic bags
whales entangled in fishing
monkey's brain at the Wuhan market
cure your impotence with rhino's horns
brumbies culled   koalas burnt   kangaroos shot
bears search for food in rubbish bins
bats without trees   rats poisoned
weedkiller kills bees   seas emptied of fish   hens in cages
sheep suffocate in boats   religion.co
cows pregnant all year   calves end in
barbecue
ivory much appreciated
turtle's shells also coveted
minks make elegant overcoats
live lobsters direct to your plate oysters as well
coronavirus rejoice because humans are on the mend

Australia

Red, ochre, vibrant soil
which like notes penetrate
not only the eyes but also the soul.
Vast land that swallows water
where ant hills appear to be
silent penitents in prayer.
Here and there native flowers
break the occasional monotony.
Sad lament of crows in flight,
they descend onto their meal,
a dead kangaroo, victim of thirst
or speeding drivers.
No chisel-sculpted rocks
just rocks which during dawn
seem to be metamorphose
into scary beings to chase
defilers of sacred places.
Dreamland of dreams to be,
where gums dress in many forms
and the soil bewitches us.
Solitude of waterholes
which, like a caring mother,
gives of herself and sustains
the ebullient life
that flourishes under the sky,
a cloudless cerulean blue,
...and then slowly
grey shapes opaque
nature's colourful narrative.

How many thousands of years
has this silver-studded shawl
covered this bejewelled land?

cogitating

i see the dry soil after the fires
on the skin of my face
i round my back like a wave
that curves towards the coast

pain   pain   pain   pain   pain

who has replaced my body
my mind is the same as when
i chased dreams and imagined fame

tired   tired   tired   tired   tired

i collect feathers from angels' wings
that bring me hope
to be what i was in times gone by

dead   dead   dead   dead   dead

dreams do not die they rest
like the winter rests in summer
i am who i was but i do not remember

truth   truth   truth   truth   truth

cataracts are not a mass of water
that falls over rocks on a mountain
they are clouds that hide the truth
a truth that hurts like a lover that cheats.

i hear but I am deaf… i speak but I am silent… i am alive but i am dead…

I am a Puppet

This sadness that envelops me
drags me down into an underworld
no light in this tunnel
only a peephole from where
I see life pass me by.

Minutes lost in minutia
moments of idleness
accumulated like trophies
hidden under blankets
sleep becomes my ally.

There is no escape
from this prison
that enslaves my soul

Eppur si muove.

My Temple

I lie on a bed
of dead moist leaves,
like Corinthian columns
gum trees adorn my cathedral.
I dream, dreams fanned
by branches, which like ballerinas
move graciously
as the wind tells me stories
from an ancient past.
No sermons or eulogies,
no chanting or prayers,
no homilies,
just cicadas singing
they tell me that tomorrow
will be another hot day.
No tapestries hang
from marble walls,
just bark with intricate patterns
made with shades of grey,
brown, black and green
colours that create pictures
where the imagination
see nature's hand at art.
Bush rocks are my sculptures
and bull ants penitents.
Freedom and peace
I pray in my refuge
while above the sky
dresses the forest
with a blue velvet cape.

I meet my creator in the crevices
of fallen trunks,
in the eucalyptus mist,
in the song of the bell bird,
in the shimmer of silver leaves,
in the determination of this
tired land which screams for survival.
Flowering grevilleas make
offerings to the native bees,
while hurried lizards pass me by.
The dry earth blesses me as I breathe solitude.

Poemario

I

How many times were you born? You asked and I replied:
'Once on a spring day many others on winter nights,' I said
but you should have asked me how many times have you died?
Did you know that each time I left this world I came back?
Every departure brought about a new life which sprouted
in a fertile ground where ashes nourished the soil. Time inexorably
passed sometimes fast like the pleasure of good things other times slowly like when I wait for your return.
I delved into eternity, crossed narrow abysses, I lost myself in memories
With the wish to survive, to emerge from chaos and confusion
I brought myself back to life. Yes, I was once born from a man and a woman
others from experience and pain. Many obscured my way…
they blinded and maimed me… In the process of living I learnt to pretend
that I had ceased to exist and to be…and you give birth to me
every time we make love or when you recite litanies to give me reasons to live.

II

We walked around the Celtic ruins, 'A burial place,' you said
and prayed.
I touched the stones and felt through my pores and veins
not death but life – a millenary life, energy shook my body
as the cold rain made my hair stick to my face.
I closed my eyes and saw them alive around the fire
women – children – the young the old chant, pace,
they conjure the pagan gods, the heathen spirits. I saw the colours
of their pots and pitchers – pregnant shapes – earthenware –
jewellery and ornaments – brilliant mandalas. Their magic
and forgotten glories imprinted in my soul which saw my pain.

III

What is love? You murmured dipping yourself
in my fervent trembly body
I turned my face to hide my tears
mute and lifeless I request forgiveness.

IV

You asked me – who are you?
I am never the same as I was yesterday
…and I change, you follow each change
as if tracing it on paper
you mould yourself to my moods and whims
while I search for an unreachable knowledge
hidden within ourselves.
How can I be the same after so many births?
Please tell me. You are the keeper of records
the answers collector, our memories holder.
Who am I? You did not answer.

Malfunction

The faulty china dolls,
baked from dust and a spark of sapient
reign in a decaying world.
A brook sings a monotonous song
obscure chanting of pebbles rattling and
at the bottom-fool's gold waiting.
A trail of dreams all the way to heaven
a maiden weave with nylon threads
a giant net to catch an eagle.
Soldiers march blindfolded and mute
to defend a dead future.
The streets are deserted, at the dinner table
families sit to a meal of images
imprisoned in a wooden box.
Humans play chess with nature
ticks bursting with blood,
fungus growing with lust.
Earthly concern: trips to the moon
a radar points to the stars,
joined by a synthetic cord
while the mind of all minds
cries at the failures
his/her creation.

Wisteria

Purple shawl that covered
the patio in spring
its tangled branches
responded to nature's
urgent mandate,
and bunches of
perfumed buds
one by one opened.
A solitary child
sat under the wisteria
dreaming of better times,
a child who learnt
that marriage alone
does not keep
parents together.
The wisteria heard
the child's prayers
making promises
to an omnipotent god
who never heard
the begging wishes.
When summer came
and the flowers died
the wisteria dressed itself
with its best green.
Would her parents
stay together?

She wondered
eyes to heaven.
Then as time passed
one by one
the brilliant leaves
turned to gold
and like miniature kites
descended onto the patio.
The bare branches,
which twisted and winded
on the metal frame
told the child
it was autumn…
The house was sold,
the suitcases packed
not only with clothes
and the memory
of the wisteria in flower.

Observatory Hill

in a vast universe
this microcosm
called Earth travels
ignoring that its past
is buried in its atoms
hidden in its layers
we are energy
that make quantum leaps
shapeless and shaped
now and then travelling matter
crosses the sky
a comet   a meteorite
what destination
what purpose
the mind wonders
are we alone

a trip to the past

following an inner call
i delved into my past
to search for the meaning
of that life which long ago
was painfully left behind
attempts to reclaim my youth
wanting to walk
on familiar roads
once again to see   touch   hear
the vague images in my mind
memories embellished by time
treasured in loneliness
for years I drowned in nostalgia
remembering…
the imprisoned.   the disappeared
the dead   the now old
poets   writers   artists
my friends…
withered flowers
of an ethereal garden
a garden forever in bloom
in my fantasy world

There Was Once a River

Brother fisherman I hope you do not eat
the fish that you catch. Do you know the river is dead?
Oil, petrol, mercury, paint and shit
float shiny slimy.
Empty Coca Cola bottles, plastic bags, containers
and a greasy film travel slowly on the mourning waters.
No swimmers, no picnics at its shore,
no children making ripples with marble pebbles.
Once perhaps lovers, in their Sunday clothes
rowed up and down from one end of town to the other.
A burned car rests on one side, and a half buried
bike for rent is a lonely reminder of what
this world ends up being if no action is taken.
Wait! There is more to cry for:
a few dirty seagulls fight for a piece of bread,
flies and maggots are having a feast
a dead cat lying in sludge is being eaten away.
No sign of caution can be seen anywhere:
NO SWIMMING OR FISHING
NO DRINKING THE RIVER WATER.
BEWARE! THE RIVER IS DEAD
… And you politicians WTF are you doing?

Winter of Our Love

We share old and half forgotten
memories which are like
yellowed pages in this
calendar of our lives.
Careful steps on the road
of this peaceful dawn
no longer we dance
or run to meet each other
we are like petals of dry flowers
put to rest between the pages
of a poetry book, but our love
is fresh and vibrant as were
our dreams and hopes.
Tired bones but lucid minds
we cry we laugh we are alive
it does not matter that one day
piece by piece we will disintegrate
into the infinite eternity
but our love will never die.

A Life Together

We met in winter
and holding hands
we shared a reality
interwoven dreams
which were like leaves
that dance in autumn.
As petals of a red bromeliad
we opened the door
to our minds and hearts
and we learnt that sombre grey
is made of black and white.
But like Uluru we remained
firm, our feet grounded
our souls ethereal.
Today fighting decay
we raise our glasses
to our eternal future.

Adelaide de la Thoreza

Educated, intelligent, a poet…
Born in Spain in agitated times
her noble father named her.
Adelaida de la Toreza
she was baptised
in a lace dress and
a gold chain around her neck.
A minister and a man of letters
he believed women like men,
deserved to be educated.
She learnt music, art and languages
in the rooms of her stately home.
Her parents love and money
made Adelaida's dreams come true
clothes, jewels, trips to Rome and Paris.
Political turmoil shaded Spain
and her father in dangerous deeds
involved himself. Misfortune and illness
brought his death. Wrapped in sadness
shortly her mother followed.
Her godmother, an English woman
refined and of fortune
to London she took Adelaide.
But someone's jealousy and envy
caused her destiny to change.
She was unjustly accused of stealing
from her dear godmother and benefactor.
To the shock of those who loved her
the verdict was 'guilty', the sentence
'Transportation to Botany Bay'.
A different life commenced
for Adelaida, the 'Spanish Convict'.

No Bread Today

a mind wrapped in conundrums
mysteries peeled like an onion
layer by layer they come out
        encounters
        tragedies
        nights of sex
all projected on a white wall
graffiti
ego disintegrated
or perhaps hidden under the debris
half remembered dreams
hopes turned to
        froth
        lint
        rotten cabbage
the full moon is hidden in a cupboard
the silver spoon hangs in the bathroom
and someone collects breadcrumbs
to feed ducks in some pond.

Free Air at the Service Station

Life hangs like an overripe fig
suspended on the end of a branch.
Tremble the children of the Books
submitted to a perilous life or is it
a test or perhaps a punishment
they suffer…
have they eaten another forbidden fruit?
Faces covered, over washed hands
a jab and a rest may bring forgiveness
to the sinners who transgress.
Plaster statues give hope to some
they pray, they kneel, they beg
because they cannot breathe.
'My horse for a cylinder of air…'

The Carpenter

Yesterday

In a bronze chest
my wood and nails
were hidden and protected.
As fast as possible I left
in search of my hammer,
the one with the silver handle
and the titanium head.
But before leaving
I blew the accumulated dust
and wrote your name on it.

Today

Please return to read me
your poems carved on rocks.
Perhaps you also are there
hidden in the coffer.
No, you are in search
of my troubled spirit,
but you won't find it
because she wonders
alone in the desert.

Tomorrow

Drink my blood
search in the small lake
made with my tears
my mouth is full of sand,
press your lips against mine
give me a nail because
I have found my hammer.

Wisdom

It is wisdom to know
but also, not to know
to believe and not believe
realities, which are delusions
of a present that does not exist.
Attachments ground us
delude our souls
in search of fulfilment.
Wants…
likes and dislikes
temporary dichotomies
that enslave souls.

Ikat

Her hands are red and swollen
she binds and dyes
multicoloured patterns
which reflect the midday sun.
She dreams of freedom
as she gently prepares
the threads to be woven,
Early in the morning
in her wicker basket
she collected flowers
berries and roots,
bark and leaves
to make the brilliant hues.
Now she moves
forward and back
changing the sherds
as she wonders
would I eat today.

Ikat fabric made using an Indonesian decorative technique in which warp or weft threads, or both, are tie-dyed before weaving.

Conundrum

I could not say when this started
neither could I say when this will finish,
it is a sort of a long, long road
with no beginning and no end.
It has been like being a seed
before being a flower and
sometimes like being a flower
before being a seed, perhaps
being the last page of a book
and at the same time the front cover.
I was old when I was born
and I was a child when I visited hell
Maybe all commenced after I had dinner
with the Gods and Thor was present,
he named me Rose, a rose with a few petals
it was then summer but without the sun
or beaches or streets or buses full of people.
It was then that I…

By the Way

she sat at the end of a dream
holding in her hands the stem
of a plastic flower
      solemn
            sad
                  simple trajectory of an angel

bathed in fury
encounter of the souls
who don't ask permission

to live
to beg
to adore
            the ones who hold the power
            the ones who control
            the ones who dominate

            the rulers

they do determine
the length of the life of the poor
      the unemployed
            the sick
and…
            plants die without water
weeds continue to grow

the miserable shed tears
mothers pray
and politicians give speeches

solace
sublime
silence of the dead

only the dead have hope

The Closed Room

Toss into the infinite
a handful of sparks
golden nuggets
silver rivers
sparkles
power
to
whom
awaits
at the end
of a rainbow
colours, brilliant
colours after the rain
direct the lost souls
to the closed door
of a room without
a window to life
lost pilgrims
hold hands
searching
for the
key.

The Universe

The universe
a convoluted idea
in the creator's mind.
Science, mathematics,
physics and music
atavistic reflections
of that original thought.
Chance has a limited number
of possible outcomes,
the range is finite.
Consciousness, feelings,
love and honour
seeds sewn at random
that now grow on grey matter.
Neutrons and electrons
atoms and galaxies
vibrate as the creator
rests after her initial push.
...and we gyrate and collide
in inner and outer space.
She created and we destroy,
trying to understand
the vast mysteries
of our souls and minds.

The Sea

Jervis Bay

Energy and solace
at the edge of the sea
the sun entering my pores
the air fanning my face.
Thoughts bundled in my mind
memories of past forgotten days.
I breathe freedom and peace…
The ever-moving mass of water
constant and persistent
reminds me of my inner search –
desperately seeking answers
amidst turmoil and chaos.
I rest on the hot sand
my body idle and numb
and I see myself as a child:
Mother holding my hand,
her control, her orders, her power
transmitted through her firm grip.
As yesterday I want to undress
and run into the blue-green water
tasting the salt in my dry mouth
letting my tears be part of the sea.
My feet eager to feel the hot sand
which will sprinkle golden specks
over my tired skinny legs.
Past and present tied together,
curious parcel wrapped in seaweed.
Not far in the sleepy bush
a lonely cricket sings for rain
as I bury a secret on an empty shell.

A Knock at the Door

Babel of a romance in chapters
bottled up emotions + emotions expressed
banned from my life   many times…
bad penny – always at my front door.
Bang! Bang! Bang! My heart goes when I see you.
Bared my soul   many times…
beaten down by your actions,
but you bedazzled me with your words.
Blame diffused, I relent   many times…

Being

Being a being that wants to be
without being or being there
being here is not being
being now, perhaps
is, being a being
being being
being

Being
being sleep
is not being
a being of the night
neither is being alive
being a being of the day
being, just being is
perhaps a dream of being.

Sadness at not being
    Resentment at not being
        Pain at not being
            Anger at not being
                Loneliness at not being
                    Mad at not being

Being a marionette is not being
being human is not being a marionette.
Being a mutant is being a mutant is being a mutant.
What form does it take to be a living being who is not a mutant?
Please let me be.

Impossible

'Impossible, we can't stop
the war in Iraq. We need petrol,
war is big business.'
'Impossible, we can't save
the Brazilian jungle, we
need the soil to breed cows,
cows that become hamburgers.'
'Impossible, we can't wave
the debt of Latin-America.'
'Impossible, we need to keep
burning fuel, for our cars,
our factories, our air-conditioners,
our '..., our...our...our...'
'Impossible, we can't take refugees.
Keep them in detention.'
'Impossible' a word in the lips
of insensitive, selfish and greedy
beings who refuse to see reality.
'Impossible' their weak excuse.

Just Born

you ask
what is this world in which I find yourself you cry
what are these noises that to my ears come? …and cry
this is a meaningless place you wonder
the senses rule sight hearing touch
you were part of a woman you cry – no tears
sad story no longer warm and floating
now you are 'one' a frightened single being
you are lost in this new life you cry
you kick you wet yourself you shit you cry again
your mother tenderly new love
upon her breast holds you velvet skin over skin
her milk soothes the pain contentment
silence all around you cry
she puts you to sleep adoring eyes
rocking you she softly sings:
will he be a prince? will he be a pauper?
will he fight wars? Will he honor peace you cry no longer.

P For Lesson Learned

parading thoughts and memories
perspective from an angle
perpetual voyage of the mind
passage of time – a life well lived
perennial flowers in the garden of love:
passions, tears, departures and encounters
persistent waves eroding rocks
pulchritude of a deserted beach
peaceful solitude and contentment.

ABPPR

a for affray
abject destiny of an intense love
abrupt departure of kindness
abandon cursory sentiments
abase your arrogance and
abstain from hate and nastiness.
absurd behaviour of a once
affectionate and kind soul.

b for knock at the door
babel of a romance in chapters
bottled up emotions + emotions expressed
banned from her life   many times…
bad penny – always at her front door.
bang! bang! bang!   her heart goes when she sees him.
bared her soul   many times…
beaten down by his actions,   many times…
but he bedazzles her with his words.
blame diffused, she relents   many times…

p for lesson learned
parading thoughts and memories
perspective from an angle
perpetual voyage of the mind
passage of time – a life well lived
perennial flowers of the garden of love:
passions, tears, departures and encounters
persistent waves eroding rocks
pulchritude of a deserted beach
peaceful solitude and contentment.
R FOR ROMANCE ENDED

Fetish

He is a smoke jumper
in his backpack he only carries
the shoes he stole
now he is ready to jump
...and he does
no food no water
only with the objects of his desire
sustenance unnecessary
the smell of smoke
penetrates him
fumes exalt his passion
he wants to be alone
he falls slowly and curses
finally touch down
the fire is small
time to deal with it after
the shoes are out
reds...his favourite colour
he smells them
caresses the soft leathers
kiss rub kiss rub kiss
....
Time to deal with the fire.

There is a Hunger

There is a hunger
that feeds on land
there is a greed
that indulges in oil
vanity that mirrors power
transgression…domination…
Banquet of horrors
tablecloth tinted in blood
innocents are not invited
to the feast of the lawless
who sit at a table
set for destruction
moping the dead
to the scrap heap.

Who Are They?

Capable of the most honourable deeds
and the cruelest of actions
contradictory beings
creators or art and music
yet some are warmongers
destroyers of lives
some build cities
gardens and parks
others efface forests and rivers
conservationists fight
philosophers and tyrants
free thinkers and demagogues
humanitarians and racists
scientists and murderers
All part of this mélange
we call humanity.

Awakening

Morning glory honeysuckle
Convolvulus Lonicera
kisses and cuddles
awakenings of the souls
embraces of the minds
the radio is playing Mahler.
A tea would be nice
for the rested bodies.
The dogs are running
up down the corridor
they also want their meal,
and the sun dances
in the front garden
waiting for Godot.

Drummoyne

She is out for her morning walk
the jacarandas have painted
her street in a cerulean blue
a carpet made of flowers
the jasmine is also in bloom
and a few grevilleas
titillate at her gentle touch
she loves to cut flowers
but she doesn't,
she caresses them
all the way to the marina,
where she imagines
that she steals a boat.
At the Rowers Club
a champagne breakfast
celebration time for someone.
She sits to watch the seagulls
being fed by a local.
The city across the stretch of water
is enveloped in summer glare
it seems a vision from the future…
she thanks her stars because
her eyes can indulge in such beauty
Drummoyne so near the sea.

escape

time knotted at her throat
like a silk scarf worn in autumn
away from reality she becomes
a winged being who flies
she extends her hands to touch
the faraway the impossible
in this space that is only hers
time does not exist
the light is subtle
accusers do not thrive
and guilt doesn't touch her
pain is only the fantasy
of a madman god believer
in this imaginary world
she is no longer a prisoner.

Making Love

I felt your hands
scattering stars
on the vault of my body.
I burned with the sun of your skin
as your tongue drew rainbows
on my agitated breast.
Your moon eyes blinded me
with its silver-blue rays.
Like angel's wings
your soft and perfumed hair
caressed my belly.
Your voice like rain
soothed my spirit,
as my mouth tasted the salt
that was offered to me.

Australiana

I want to have a history attached to this country
a history that ties me to ancestors born on this land
I want a convict great-grandparent, or a swagman,
or an uncle poet who wrote about the bush.
I want sepia-colored photos of relatives
working on a station. I want to talk about
my father fighting in France, and of his father
buried in Gallipoli, I want a mother
who told me about rations and the depression
about the Japs and the bombing of Darwin.
I long to have had a childhood in the suburbs
with weekends of barbecues and games of cricket.
I want to know primary school songs, and reunions
with friends from my adolescence. I want a shared past.
I want people to see me not just a migrant
I want to be more than an Australian at heart.

Writing Poetry

sometimes i believe
that everything has been said
that publishers don't want poetry
that no one reads poetry
that poetry is dead

sometimes i do believe
that there are things to say
but what if i am wrong
no i found 26,900,000
entries re poetry in google

yet there is a compulsion
yet there is an obsession
yet there is a passion
that impulses me to write

can't stop writing
learning new words
searching for new meanings
verses and more verses

i have an idea of myself
i have an image
i have a role in life
I write write write

a woman of rhythm
a poet
a wordsmith
born with a pen in my hand

Words will accompany to my death
i lived always with ink stains
verses written on dockets
on paper tablecloths
reciting poetry
in my head
to a public
later to
you.

Soul Healers

To the counsellors at the NSW Rape Crisis Centre

As there are perpetrators
there are others who care
those whom with warmth
in their eyes and empathy
understand the pain
of women raped
those who with kindness
pronounce words of hope.
Loving women
who undo the damage
done by perpetrators.
Dedicated humans
who restore faith,
and the will to live.
Devoted beings
who replenish
the essence of the wounded,
paving the roads
with cobbles of optimism.
Restorers of sanity –
menders of the mind.

Existing

Let me be you for a moment
at peace with yourself
in the long dark nights
of this eternal travel
through the universe.
Where am I? Guide me
through this tunnel
leading towards a garden
where sincerity flowers
contentment and love grow
like gardenias in your garden.
You know your way
teach me I lost my destination
He took me by the hand
and we entered a world
described in ones and zeros
abstract concepts
symbols of eternity.
We wondered in the space
between sky and earth
where the silence
slapped my face
like my mother's hand.
I was wrong.

Divorce

She is the shadow that enters his empty room
She is the knife that wants to pierce his heart
She is the lonely soul that rests in the dark
She is one of the discarded many…

Perhaps also she is
a beggar
a looser
a bee sting
a blister in his foot.

…and till death do us apart was said

She scribbles words
She recites words
She prays words
and that is all they are just words
empty valueless useless.

In another life
in another time
they savoured togetherness
they drank their essences
they bathed under the moon
they were
like stone and chisel
like veins and blood
like food and mouth.

The last remnants of his presence
an old toothbrush and a faint perfume
left in the wardrobe which reminds her
that he was not a dream.

Secure

I escaped from a nightmare,
persecuted by my memories
breathless I run – panic
my existence denied.
harassed by my guilt
and ashamed I hid
under the moon of your skirt.
From that secure place
I learnt to confront
phantoms and insecurities
while with your tongue
you wrote 'I love you'
on my trembling breast.

The Void

Parallel existences in a shared nightmare
pariahs of sombre and empty lives
isolated from each other and yet together.
Obtuse cacophony of their dreams
pathetic cadence of their love murmurs
they are in a virtual reality program
packed with incongruent events
sometimes feelings of pain and pleasure.
There are forces that repel and compel each other
worlds that clash in space, elliptical orbits
that brings them to a forbidden ritual.
A distorted reality in their minds,
they travel through time and space.
Elementals, zombies, animas…
A sense of loss and emptiness
pervade their beings
confusion, chaos, abashment,
entanglement of emotions. Solitude.
They are holograms, random shapes,
denizens, figures projected on a screen,
They are survivors in a dead world
engaged in a charade of hollow acts.

The End of the Road

she hides her shame under the shade of the trees
in her mind an echo   twitter of birds
impending madness
the sky embraces her   an ominous blanket

useless gold she carries in her pocket
glitter in her heart   she follows a dirt road
her solitude she cherishes   swallows her pain
she chased those around her like a currawong
chatter in her brain   forget   forget   forget

she wants to follow a straight path
her steps take her to a hollow labyrinth.
she strokes her cat to find peace   temporary solace
in a glass of whisky   all forgotten.

Tricks

in her mind the woman traced a window on the wall
through it she saw herself embracing a child
bathed in shadows she crossed herself
forgotten childhood memories emerged
eating eggs just collected from the nesting box
admiring Van Gogh *Undergrowth* in Amsterdam
suddenly a distraction – the sound of water running
a tap opened perhaps? A platinum-coloured figure
stood there observing her, rocks appear to tumble down
from the top of her wardrobe, she closed her eyes
and saw shinning eyes, sparkling shapes
her heart accelerated and she gave another puff
of her weed cigarette, was it morning or night?
She believed she was unscathed by the past
but the wounds were there like shutters to life

lobotomy

the will to act
survives injury after injury after injury
the power to feel
hinges humans to the world
despite the incursions
of the inner beast
which attracts us
to the splendour of deformities
which obscures the path
to a shallow end
unchain the soul out of itself
scour the impurities
ignore the stench
come float in self-esteem
engulf yourself
with the passion for art
be sea be waves be tides
stop the rot in the frontal lobe

resurrection

she traces a line   on an imaginary paper
which rests on a table   the past a hollow memory
she writes and dreams to be at the banks of a river
tears   tears   tears   no notion of time
float   flow   flourish   creates a new character of herself
double her strength   she will learn to love herself
the race has begun   yet she anchors her body to the ground
her face and lips are dry   her bones made of dust
is she a ghost   no   she can prove she is alive
clothes cover her body   her feet are in boots
her anxiety embraced the night   dread   loneliness
the moonlight casts a shape on the bare walls
what does she hold in her hands   ash   dust
decisions made   no bullshit   hope
the imaginary paper glides   she created the wind.

a voice heard

you are   at the foot of a mountain
a mountain   with scars
scars   that flavour the mood
mood   peremptory as rust
rust   which echoes guilt
guilt   without words
words   an aeolian process   like dust
dust   on your skin   wake up
wake up   wake up   not a dream
break   the carnivorous feelings   weak
weak being   you want
want   want   want
the truth   you don't know what you want

dead

no sound   no pain   numb
hands in prayer position
a cardboard box surrounds me
am i dead   yet I can see
a rope around my neck
have I killed myself

scream   scream   scream
no words come out
is this my forever position
guilt   repentance
prayers   absolution
have I gone through that bullshit

i am a non-believer
have i been punished
no angels on clouds
who sing to the powerful
god of the heavens

someone shakes me
screaming in my ear
wake up   wake up   wake up

ego conflagration

sucked between two worlds I
sucked the blood of the future

lost on the periphery searching for
lost objects in the restricted space

eternity was so far away
eternity was then just a word

dry skin dry soul dry self
dry of feelings   just dry

north of everything alone
north of where you were

ad infinitum promises
ad infinitum hope

dead like the poems of Agathon
dead like that which started

fooled by the sound of your music
fooled by the stars you showered on me

polarisation

souls entangled like wisteria branches
a path unfollowed   mysterious encounter
arms extended to touch the infinite
absorbed by the expansion   love predicted
nights protracted secrets revealed
present yet absent   ironies of destiny
a photon split-positron-pair annihilation
existence doubted   reality questioned
yet their bodies merged in an embrace
quandary   choices suspended
morality versus love versus passion
dense perplexity   riddles conundrums
intricate patterns of behaviour
mystic attachment   ego dissolved
the intellect bypassed just being one

enslaved

without realising it i entered a world
that absorbed me and made me the slave
of a hungry master that devoured
hours and hours and hours & left me with
numb fingers foggy brain isolated
frustrated forced to make sequences
demanded by the monster
these must be in perfect
systematic order
otherwise failure
yet I love it
solitaire

sing the blues with me

images flying
flimsy flat flippant
they undulate languidly
in her feverish mind
for a moment they rest
actors in a delusion
they seat to drink tea
on non-existent chairs
one stands up and sings
hoochie coochie man
she takes another pill
falls asleep
dreams of the dead
playing cards on
an out of tune piano

and now what

WAR
no resolutions no peace no armistice
broken romance hostile relationship
armies maraud – oppression
land in exchange for life – desolation
W A R
false patriotism denies pity ignores pain
epaulets pride   prejudicial judgements
demagogues with irrational arguments
rhetorically exploit naïve minds
obtain uncontested power no dissent

W A R
fire noises sirens tanks
guns   bombs   injuries
death bloodshed combat
conflict strife abuse greed
W A R
contest   dust-up   fracas
fray   struggle   dispute
confrontation contretemps
logomachy crossfire
rape refugees prisoners

WAR
pleasure seeking hedonistic oligarchs
oblivious to carnage blind to struggles
soldiers – human *Pithovirus sibericum*

W A R
hostilities disruption
hunger isolation hate
malevolence bitterness

sleepwalkers trained to kill escape hide strike numb
and now what

the prophets/politicians/profits

words produced without real meaning
answers given because they were demanded
crude sounds vague and false responses
unbalanced equilibrium   culpable reason
to see the fire burn of a differential criterion
validity created by people who fall into the power trap
can we recognise ourselves in those
who govern and create the rules
hope is hidden like a miser hides his riches
paupers count crumbs and the homeless
steal corners under a blanket
those who shamelessly fornicate the present
continue consulting the oracle
yet the truth is there for all to see

accumulation

i have collected words
like others collect gold
or stamps or coins
securely treasured
in the vaults of my memory
admired prisoners
cherished jewels
that I thread in sentences
words are my beginning
my end my substance

words
flowers in my garden of pages
words
the sword of my battles
words
the poison of my anger
words
for healing those who suffer
words
to soothe the pain

words to love

a dead garden

passion eroded
like the desert of Atacama
tenderness   deflowered
like   a   virgin   raped
passion   drowned
friendship   mutilated
anger reigns in the country
of   their   bodies
memories of embraces
metamorphose
killing desire
repugnance
rejection
yet…

chrysalis

he tied her legs
with bunches of roses
her hands he imprisoned
with love letters
the heart that palpitated
in the tortured body
with jealousy he pierced
and with his fist
he stamped possession
while he claims
'it's your fault'
he can abuse and punish her
but one day
her eyes opened to reality
the prison of make-believe love
filled with valour she escapes
confidence regained
she marches head high
a new woman
who no one owns

searching for answers

the truth wrapped in silver foil
words silenced like those of a prisoner
nothing said   no excuses
gated utterances   unable to escape
forces that drive denialism
paradigm   asserting the natural
accumulation of critical anomalies
relationship of shifting parameters
broad sweep of measured reality
deplorable mundane alternatives
tired of the usual narratives
of power and triumphalism
dispassionate   cold   myopic
ingrained desire to make sense
of the 'messages in a bottle'

the sum of others

ancestral designs
printed on cells
women' mitochondria
leading the way
patterns of behaviours
travelling through time
encoded messages
flowing in our blood
likes and dislikes
choosing this path
or another one
preferences attractions
are these our decisions
written in the past
is the scroll of life

Ad Infinitum

Tender love of ancient souls
they share old and tired dreams
yellowed pages in this calendar
of lives long lived…
Careful steps on the road
of this peaceful dawn
petals of dry flowers
flowers which one day
were as fresh as their hopes.
Tired bones lucid minds
with treasured memories
which in time will be forgotten
one by one piece by piece
will disintegrate into what?

www.ingramcontent.com/pod-product-compliance
Lightning Source LLC
Chambersburg PA
CBHW071031080526
44587CB00015B/2569